SOME OF THE OTHER PUBLICATIONS BY DR. CHRIS BART, FCA

Sex, lies and mission statements

Developing Mission Statements which Work

Industrial Firms and the Power of Mission

The Impact of Mission on Firm Innovativeness

Mission Possible

Mission Matters

Making Mission Statements Count

Accepting the Mission

Lasting Inspiration

Who's Running the Store?

A Tale of Two Employees and the person who wanted to lead them.

The Relationship Between Mission Statements and Firm Performance: An Exploratory Study

Exploring the Application of Mission Statements on the Internet

Measuring the mission effect in human intellectual capital

Innovation, Mission Statements and Learning

A Comparison of Mission Statements and their Rationales in Innovative and Non-Innovative Firms

Distinguishing Between the Board and Management in Company Mission: Implications for Corporate Governance

Mission statements in Canadian Hospitals

Mission Statement Content and Hospital Performance in the Canadian Not-for-Profit Health Care Sector

Mission Statement Rationales and Organizational Alignment in the Not-for-profit Healthcare Sector

Mission Statements in Canadian Not-for-Profit Hospitals: Does Process Mattter?

A Model of the Impact of Mission Rationale, Content, Process and Alignment on Firm Performance

The governance role of the board in strategy: An initial progress report

The Governance Role of the Board in Corporate Strategy: A Comparison of Board Practices in 'For Profit' and 'Not-for-profit' Organizations

An Empirical Examination of the Content and Composition of Board Charters

Issues in Canadian Board Transparency

A comparative analysis of mission statement content in secular and faith based hospitals

High-Tech Firms: Does Mission Matter?

Mission Use and Innovation in the Airline Industry: An Exploratory Investigation

Improving the board's involvement in corporate strategy: Directors speak out

Leveraging Human Intellectual capital through an Employee Volunteer Program and Service-Learning: The Case of Ford Motor Company of Canada

The Role of the Board in IT Governance: Current and Desired Oversight Practices

The following are just a few of the organizations Dr. Bart has helped:

Financial Services

- Bank of Montreal
- TD Canada Trust
- Deloitte & Touche
- CFO Financial Executives Forum
- Australian Society of Accountants
- State Farm Insurance

Health Care

- Ontario Hospital Association
- BC Health Leaders Forum
- Trillium Health Centre
- Credit Valley Hospital
- McMaster University Medical Centre
- The Griffin Centre

Government

- Treasury Board Secretariat
- Canadian Embassy, Washington, D.C.
- Nova Scotia Public Service Long Term Disability Plan
- Saskatchewan Research Council
- The Corporation of the Town of Oakville
- Office of the Superintendent of Financial Institutions

Services and Manufacturing

- ArcelorMittal Dofasco
- SAP
- Kraft Foods
- CBC Inc.
- CarSTAR Collision Service
- Apple Auto Glass

Human Resources

- Human Resources Professionals Association
- Canadian Human Resource Planners
- International Air Transport Association
- Conference Board of Canada
- Ontario Pharmacists' Association
- Association of Canadian Port Authorities

Education

- University of Western Ontario
- McMaster University
- University of Waterloo
- Mount Saint Vincent University
- Canadian Assoc. for Co-operative Ed.
- University of North Texas

20
ESSENTIAL QUESTIONS
DIRECTORS OF NOT-FOR-PROFIT ORGANIZATIONS SHOULD ASK ABOUT STRATEGY

and Workbook

Dr. Chris Bart, FCA

The world's leading authority on mission and vision statements and their successful implementation.

Author of the Best Selling CICA publication,
20 Questions Directors Should Ask About Strategy, 2nd Edition

For Judy, with love

Copyright © 2009 Chris Bart

All rights resrved. No part of this book may be used
or reproduced in any manner whatsoever without written permission
except in the case of brief quotations used in critical articles or reviews.

Dr. Chris Bart, FCA
Corporate Missions Inc.
1063 King Street West, Suite 230
Hamilton, ON Canada L8S 4S3
905-308-8455
chrisbart@corporatemissionsinc.com
www.corporatemissionsinc.com

ISBN: 978-0-9732247-3-3

Design and composition by John Reinhardt Book Design

Contents

Preface 7

How to Use this Publication 9

Not-for-profit Directors and Strategy 11

20 Questions Not-for-profit Directors Should Ask About Strategy 15

Appendices

  Appendix 1: Strategy at "Theatre Capricorn" 35

  Appendix 2: Strategy at "The Prairie Club" 39

  Appendix 3: Strategy at "Save the World Foundation" 41

  Appendix 4: Strategy at "St. Alexandra's Hospital" 43

  Appendix 5: Strategic Plans and Planning 47

20 Questions Workbook 49

About the Author 57

Preface

THIS MONOGRAPH is designed to help members of not-for-profit boards fulfill their responsibility for contributing to the development of their organization's strategic direction and for approving and monitoring the strategic plan. It is intended primarily to help individual directors, but boards may also wish to use it for orientation and discussion.

The role of not-for-profit directors sometimes includes actually formulating the organization's strategic plan—especially where smaller scale organizations are concerned. More often though, when sufficient staff resources are available, it involves participating with staff to help set the mission, vision and values and then constructively engaging with them to gain reasonable assurance (by asking enough of the right kinds of questions) that the rest of the plan has been properly developed and is, in fact, plausible. This monograph provides suggested questions for boards to ask the CEO or Executive Director, senior management, professional advisors—and even itself. For each question there is a brief explanatory background.

The text includes references to other titles.

Chris Bart

How to Use this Publication

THIS PUBLICATION is designed to be a concise, easy-to-read introduction to the role that directors play in performing one of their most important functions—**helping to set the strategic direction of the organization**. The question format reflects the oversight role of directors, which includes asking management—and themselves—questions to fulfill their primary fiduciary responsibility i.e. **to act in the best interests of the organization and *all* of its stakeholders, not just one or more selected stakeholder groups**. Unfortunately, in the past, not all not-for-profit directors felt comfortable in asking questions in the boardroom, often because they didn't know what types of questions to ask—and which ones were even permissible.

Accordingly, the questions presented here offer guidance to not-for-profit directors on frameworks, processes and outcomes in order both to provide them with insight and to stimulate discussion on the important topics related to strategy. These questions however are not intended to be a comprehensive checklist—they are merely a starting point. *But, they are also questions for which the answers should be known by every not-for-profit director.*

It should be pointed out that, in some cases, asking these questions directly of management may not always be the preferred course of action. In such circumstances, then, the board should ask management to prepare briefings that address the salient points raised by the questions.

Finally, the comments that accompany the questions in this monograph are intended to provide directors with a basis for critically assessing the answers they are given and for digging deeper if necessary. The comments summarize current thinking on the issues and the practices of leading not-for-profit organizations. And while the questions can—and should—apply to any not-for-profit organization, the answers will naturally vary according to the size, complexity and sophistication of each individual organization.

Not-for-profit Directors and Strategy

WHAT IS THE RESPONSIBILITY of not-for-profit boards for their organization's strategy and what should it be?

At its most general level, a board's responsibility for strategy stems from the simple fact that *all* not-for-profit organizations are created to fulfill some purpose and that, over time, this purpose may change. While that purpose may be for some social cause ("to make the world a better place") or simply to meet the needs of some sort of "association" or charity, the people who contribute financially (or in kind) to the organization—donors, sponsors, funders, members and volunteers—all want to feel confident that their offerings and support are not going to be squandered or misused.

Boards of directors, therefore, have been created to be the legal "stewards" of an organization.

What this means in practical terms is that directors have been entrusted with the assets of the organization and, therefore, are responsible for their *safeguarding, enhancing their value and/or appropriately distributing them.* Stewardship also means, though, that boards are responsible for ensuring that the affairs of the organization are managed in accordance with its stated purpose either directly or by delegating this responsibility to one or more managers and then 'supervising' them.

Accordingly, directors need to be selected with care and their responsibilities need to be taken seriously. In particular, they should be selected on the basis of their ability to provide the organization with **oversight, insight and foresight.**

In terms of their 'oversight' function, directors must ensure that appropriate attention is given to the organization's strategy as well as identifying, managing and monitoring risks. The oversight role also involves providing for the smooth, effective and efficient functioning of the organization.

With respect to their 'insight' role, not-for-profit boards are expected to add their experience and wisdom to improve the organization's performance. Directors of smaller not-for-profits, for example, are typi-

cally required by necessity to take a more hands-on role such as when a director with financial expertise is also asked to serve as the organization's treasurer. On the other hand, when professional managers are in place, directors use their insight capabilities to supplement and enhance (but *not* second guess) executive decision-making.

As for 'foresight', not-for-profit organizations want their directors to provide a perspective on the future that helps the organization identify those opportunities that are most worth pursuing.

But, whether or not they delegate responsibility for managing the organization to others, the ultimate goal for directors to seek in their pursuit of good governance is *the promotion of effective decision making*. Directors are there to make sure that the right decisions are made on a timely basis. And of all the decisions that a board might be called upon to make or approve, one of the most important concerns the selection of the organization's strategy.

Interestingly, the nature and degree of a board's actual participation in **creating, reviewing and approving** their organization's strategy will vary with the circumstances in which the directors find themselves.

For example, many not-for-profit organizations are relatively small in size and operate with an extremely focused local mandate. In such circumstances, there may be few paid support staff and the organization typically lacks managerial depth. Therefore, the task of performing many, if not all, of the organization's managerial functions usually falls on the shoulders of the directors. In these organizations, the board's responsibility for strategy involves both formulating the strategy and creating the written document that describes it—i.e., the strategic plan. And then there is the additional burden of developing a detailed operating plan and budget to bring the strategy to life. Consequently, being a responsible director in these situations can be a lot of work. This, perhaps, is a reason why many smaller not-for-profit organizations find it is so hard to find—and keep—good directors.

On the other hand, boards of larger not-for-profit organizations generally share their involvement in strategy with the professional managers who perform the day-to-day work of the organization (and who also have the job of turning the strategy into an operating plan and then executing it). In these circumstances, the board's job is to lay down a structure and process that allows it to be *constructively involved* with management in both developing and approving the organization's strategy.

Constructive involvement

A major consideration in becoming constructively involved concerns the specification of the division of responsibilities between the board and management for the various tasks undertaken to lead the organization. One recommended way of organizing a board's constructive involvement

in relation to developing strategy is provided in Figure F1. This template, however, anticipates a medium to large not-for-profit organization in which the board stays focused exclusively on strategic issues and leaves responsibility for operations exclusively in the hands of management.

Naturally, in smaller not-for-profits, where the directors have a hands-on role in the day-to-day management of the organization, the board's operational responsibilities will increase and also trigger the need for the board to divide its operational and supervisory responsibilities among its members.

For constructive involvement to be truly effective, however, a culture and climate of mutual respect and trust must exist between the board and senior management. This is something the board and management are both responsible for creating. For its part, the board contributes to building this culture by making sure that it participates in setting strategy in a cooperative rather than confrontational manner.

At the core of constructive involvement, however, is the role that directors perform through *the questions they ask either of management or of themselves*. By asking questions, ideally with fresh and unbiased eyes, directors aim to determine whether the organization:

- ✓ is on a proper course
- ✓ conducting optimal decision making (as opposed to "satisficing" i.e., accepting decisions that are just "good enough")
- ✓ exercises sufficient creativity in its problem solving, and
- ✓ is appropriately administered and controlled.

But not just any questions will do. When it comes to strategy, directors must ask the right questions if they are to be effective in helping the organization set a future direct'ion that will ensure its long-term survival. Indeed, doing so is the essence of all strategic planning efforts and the winning strategies that such planning efforts aspire to produce!

When developing a not-for-profit's strategy, it is especially important that the board and management consider a wide range of **stakeholders** and their viewpoints, including donors, funders, employees, volunteers, customers and communities, beneficiaries etc. After all, it is those stakeholders' response to—and support of—the strategy that is often critical to the organization's success. In so doing, however, boards must never lose sight of the fact that they **owe their primary—and fiduciary—responsibility to the organization as a whole and not to any one particular stakeholder group**.

The following table provides a framework for dividing the responsibilities for the organization's strategy and strategic planning between the board and management. The precise division of responsibilities will depend on the organization's size, complexity and resources, so each organization should determine the planning responsibilities based on the nature of the organization, the composition of the board, and any specific regulatory requirements.

FIGURE 1

Constructive Involvement: Roles and responsibilities of boards and management for strategic plans and planning

TASK	RESPONSIBILITY	
	Mgt.	Board
Developing a strategic planning process	X	
Assessing and approving the strategic planning process		X
Developing the mission, vision, and values (*)	X	X
Assessing and approving the mission, vision and values		X
Developing the objectives	X	
Assessing and approving the objectives		X
Identifying the scope of activities and domain selections	X	
Assessing and approving the scope of activities and domain selections		X
Data collection and analysis with respect to the strategic plan (See Appendix 4)	X	
Preparing the written strategic plan	X	
Assessing and approving the strategic plan		X
Scheduling strategic planning and strategy review meetings	X	
Preparing operating plans	X	
Preparing budgets	X	
Approving budgets		X
Preparing reports on the organization's strategic progress and accomplishment of strategic objectives	X	
Monitoring the execution of the strategy and its achievement		X
Approving changes to the strategy as warranted		X

* Traditional governance models restrict the board's involvement to reviewing and approving the mission, vision and values. However, recent research by the author suggests that superior organizational performance and innovativeness occurs when boards participate more actively in developing these strategic documents.

Questions Not-for-profit Directors Should Ask About Strategy

THE FOLLOWING SET of **20 Essential Questions** represents a structured framework to help not-for-profit directors fulfill their responsibilities for developing, assessing, approving, monitoring and changing their organization's strategy.

The nine questions in the first section, "In the Beginning…Understanding Strategy," will help directors develop a common understanding of strategy in the context of their own organization—**a strategic framework.** This provides the foundation needed for a more detailed discussion and assessment of their organization's strategy, using questions 10 through 20.

While the questions are presented in a particular order, individual directors may prefer to begin at different points within the framework.

It is strongly recommended, though, that directors consider all of the questions.

Finally, as with any major organizational undertaking such as determining the board's role in strategy, it is usually best to go slowly and to keep things simple. After all, most boards are usually currently involved with their organization's strategy in some fashion. Adjusting to the approach recommended here, though, may involve some major changes in the way that the board and individual directors conduct themselves. And that, in turn, may take some time to get right.

It is better to know some of the questions than all of the answers.

—James Thurber

In the Beginning…Understanding Strategy

The first question that every not-for-profit director must ask in order to grasp their organization's strategy is:

1. How is strategy defined at this organization?

While this question is easy to ask, agreeing on the answer is often difficult. Many different definitions of strategy exist and, as a result, directors often come to their organizations with different and competing

versions of the term. When combined with management's own definitions, there is often much confusion and conflict as to what constitutes the proper description of an organization's strategy.

Rather than present and debate alternative definitions, this document has adapted one recent and contemporary description of strategy, which appears to strike the balance that many directors seem to be looking for. This definition contends that formulating and articulating a strategy involves:

1. the determination of those long term *goals* (i.e., mission, vision and values) and *objectives* which reflect:
   a. the relationship that the organization wishes to have with its different stakeholder groups and,
   b. in particular, how the organization intends to address important stakeholder needs; and
2. the identification of the *scope (or domain) of activities* within which those goals and objectives are to be achieved. (adapted from: "Lasting inspiration," *CA Magazine*, May, 2000, pp. 49–50)

While other definitions exist, this approach to strategy is easily understood by any director or senior officer. It answers the **essential questions** of strategy that should be of concern to every director, which are:

Trying to predict the future is like trying to drive down a country road at night with no lights while looking out the back window.

—Peter Drucker

2. **What are we ultimately trying to accomplish (currently) and where do we eventually want to get to? (The Vision Goal)**

3. **What is our current purpose—or, why do we exist? (The Mission Goals)**
   a. Who are the key stakeholders that have a significant impact on our organization and its sustainability (i.e. users/beneficiaries, applicants, customers, paid employees/staff, volunteers, funders (e.g., owners, members, government departments, donors), society-at-large, etc.)?
   b. What specific needs are we trying to satisfy for each of our stakeholders in order to secure their long-term loyalty, commitment and support?

4. **What are the current internal ethical and cultural ("how we do things around here") priorities that attract stakeholders to us? (The Values Goals)**

5. **What are the specific measures and targets that we use to judge our progress in achieving our vision, mission and values goals? (The Objectives)**

6. **What specific product, service, benefit or assistance activities have we currently chosen to focus on and, to which specific group(s) (or markets) have we chosen to offer them for the purposes of achieving our objectives? (The Scope of Activities and Domain Selections)**
    a. *Who and/or where are our users, customers, clients, beneficiaries or target audience?*
    b. *What products, services, benefits and/or assistance do we provide to them?*

These detailed questions specify the *salient* components—vision, mission, values, objectives and scope of activities—that define and describe any organization's strategy in a **complete and comprehensive fashion**. Therefore, directors need to consider them both individually and as a group whenever they seek to describe the strategy for their particular not-for-profit organization.

Interestingly, questions 2–6 are sometimes summarized in profit-oriented companies through the more general query of "what business are we in?" Recent experience suggests, however, that using such an approach may now be too vague to gain the sort of insights that directors of profit-oriented companies are looking for.

Whatever approach is taken, though, *directors must agree among themselves and with management on how they will define and articulate the organization's strategy.*

This common understanding is necessary if everyone is to know clearly **which decisions are strategic, and which ones are not**. Failing to agree on the way strategy is defined and articulated usually results in poor communication, confusion and even conflict whenever the topic of the organization's strategy is raised. Therefore, one important contextual question that every director must ask early on with respect to assessing and approving the organization's strategy is:

If you don't know where you are going, you'll probably wind up someplace else.

—Anon.

7. **Is the definition of strategy in this not-for-profit organization shared by all directors and management?**

The definition of strategy provided on page 14 is very robust and covers a variety of circumstances. It can be used to describe any organization's strategy, whether it is one currently in place—or one being proposed for the future. Appendices 1 through 4 present examples of the strategy statements of four not-for-profit organizations: Theatre Capricorn (a regional theatre), The Prairie Club (a private members downtown business establishment), Save the World Foundation (an environmental protection NGO), and St. Alexandra's Hospital (a metropolitan medical facility). Though the examples are all real, the names have been disguised.

The definition of strategy prescribed in this document may also be used to describe two terms that are often used interchangeably, but which sometimes have quite different meanings in not-for-profit enterprises: **the business strategy and the organizational (or overall) strategy**. Generally speaking, the distinction between these two concepts turns largely on the breadth and scale of a not-for-profit's scope or domain of activities and operations.

More specifically, a business strategy usually concerns a specific product, service, benefit or activity that the organization offers to a certain type of user, customer, beneficiary or target audience in a defined location. For most small not-for-profit organization's, the scope or domain of activities is relatively narrow and they tend to provide a single benefit to one type of user in a single location. (An example of such a not-for-profit is an organization whose purpose is solely to provide meals to seniors living in a single residential home.) Because these organizations have just one business activity, their 'business strategy' would be virtually the same as their 'organizational strategy'.

Larger organizations, on the other hand, may have a variety of different activities, with a distinct business strategy for each. Directors of larger organizations with substantive, diversified activities, therefore, need to ask:

8. What are the major business strategies that make up the not-for-profit's organizational strategy?

Over time, a not-for-profit organization may provide new products, services or benefits or serve a different range of users, customers or beneficiaries. As a not-for-profit expands its activities, multiple business strategies may come into play (each defined using the strategic components provided in questions 2 though 6). Taken together, these business strategies represent the *overall* organizational strategy. The organizational strategy, therefore, becomes something separate and distinct from the individual business strategies.

In organizations with multiple business strategies, the board should focus primarily on the overall organizational strategy. It should only become involved with assessing and approving individual business strategies when they represent major changes to the organization's overall direction—such as, when a new major activity is added or an existing

one stopped. It is still advisable, though, that directors be periodically informed of and review the major business strategies so they better understand the impact these have on the whole organization.

9. Do circumstances warrant the board's involvement in (i.e. reviewing, assessing and approving) the organization's operating plan?

The operating plan puts "flesh and bones" on a not-for-profit organization's strategy. Typically, it addresses all of the major functional areas, such as marketing, finance, human resources and member/donor relations. Therefore, developing such a plan involves considering a number of specific details and **action plans** (typically referred to as **tactics**) concerning the way the organization intends to achieve its mission, vision, values and objectives.

In large not-for-profit organizations, many staff members and individual departments normally contribute to developing the operating plan. It is a process that usually involves several functional experts and requires making innumerable decisions that typically go well beyond the knowledge, competence and time availability of most directors.

Consequently, the reason why boards of larger organizations should not get involved in the details of the operating plans is fairly straightforward: *this is what management is hired and paid to do*. The board should, therefore, diligently avoid reviewing, assessing and approving the details of the organization's operating plan unless it is given specific responsibility for managing it.

Instead, directors should focus on specifying the guidelines (such as spending or policy limits) that will shape and affect the development of the operating plan. They should also ensure that operating plans are being carried out in a fiscally prudent manner as part of their normal oversight responsibilities. (For example, the board may do this through its review and approval of the organization's budget and subsequent variance reviews.)

Except for these high level reviews and summary budget approvals, the responsibility for a large not-for-profit organization's operating plan usually falls outside the board's normal governance responsibilities. However, there are still certain occasions when boards of larger not-for-profits may become actively involved in the organization's operating plan. One occurs when the organization faces a crisis and requires whatever benefit the board's collective wisdom has to offer. The other is when there is agreement *from* senior management concerning the board's involvement in this area.

Boards of smaller not-for-profit organizations, on the other hand, face different circumstances. Their organizations typically lack the support staff with significant managerial depth, so board members often take a hands-on role in managing the organization, including the review of every aspect of operations. In some circumstances, these boards may assign certain directors the responsibility for actually creating the operating plan. However, it is imperative that these boards determine how they will also carry out their governance oversight roles.

One way of doing this is by dividing various responsibilities among the directors with some having the job of providing oversight to those (other directors) who have been given the task of creating various aspects of the operating plan. For example, the board may ask a director with financial knowledge to take on an operational role as the organization's treasurer. But because the board also has a responsibility for supervising management, it may form a finance subcommittee, made up of other directors, whose role is to review and monitor the activities of the director who serves as the organization's treasurer.

Assessing and Evaluating Strategy

Once the hurdle of *describing* and understanding an organization's strategy has been navigated, the board and its directors are faced with their most important question:

10. Does this not-for-profit organization have the right strategy and, if not, what should it be?

Every organization has a strategy, which may be either explicit or implicit. However, not every organization necessarily has a good one. Given the board's responsibility for reviewing, assessing and approving the organization's strategy, it is incumbent upon directors to do their utmost to ensure that their organization's strategy is the right one for it.

The first step in assessing a not-for-profit organization's strategy is to have it formally written down and communicated explicitly to all board members (ideally by answering Questions 2–6). This allows directors the opportunity to adequately reflect upon and ponder the *choices of goals, objectives and scope of activities imbedded within that strategy*.

11. What process was used to formulate the strategy contained in the not-for-profit's strategic plan and does the plan's document contain all of the proper information?

One of the first things to consider when attempting to determine the quality and appropriateness of an organization's strategy is the way it was developed. Was the strategy developed through an orderly and thoughtful process? Or was it put together through "gut feel" and an

> *"However beautiful the strategy, you should occasionally look at the results."*
>
> —Sir Winston Churchill 1874–1965)

"on-the-back-of-an-envelope" approach? Research has confirmed that organizations that follow an organized, structured planning process develop better strategies and achieve higher performance results, on average, than those that do not.

So what is *strategic planning*?

Simply put, **strategic planning is the process that helps establish the organization's strategy**. It results in a formal, written document, referred to **as the strategic plan**.

A good strategic plan sets forth:

- ✓ The basis upon which the organization's mission, vision, values and objectives were chosen
- ✓ The reasons why the organization's scope of activities—and the markets it chooses to serve—represent the optimal choices for it to achieve its goals and objectives
- ✓ Assumptions made about the external environment that may affect the organization's ability to achieve its goals and objectives
- ✓ Assumptions made about the organization's own resources that may affect its ability to serve its external markets
- ✓ Assessments of the risks facing the organization and its strategic choices, and the way those risks are to be managed, and
- ✓ The rational for all major organizational arrangements, such as structure, staffing and controls, which are necessary for the organization to implement its strategy.

Appendix 5 provides a more detailed list of the information that should typically be produced by a good strategic planning process.

The following nine questions are provided to help directors assess the quality of the strategy presented to them and the planning process used to develop it. Directors should be satisfied that each of these questions is sufficiently answered in the plan documentation:

> *It's not the plan that is important, it's the planning.*
>
> —Dr. Graeme Edwards

12. Does the strategy have the right vision?

Visions help provide a long-term direction to an organization and enhance its stakeholders' understanding of what the organization is ultimately trying to accomplish. Generally, visions of not-for-profits are concerned with achieving greatness on one or more dimensions—be it, social outcomes, reputation, or admiration, to name just a few.

A great vision is also often an aspirational statement in which the ability—or way—to achieve it is neither readily apparent nor available. This is because the essential purpose of a vision is to describe a future state that is so desirable that it harnesses both the intellectual and emotional commitment of major stakeholders and makes them want to work towards achieving it.

Perception is strong and sight weak. In strategy it is important to see distant things as if they were close and to take a distanced view of close things.

—Miyamoto Musashi, 1584-1645, legendary Japanese swordsman

A notable example of an aspirational vision comes from the early 1960s, when US President John Kennedy challenged NASA to: "land a man on the surface of the moon and return him safely back to earth before the end of the decade." At the time, few people in NASA actually believed that was possible because it would require so many new technologies that had yet to be invented at that time. Nevertheless, Kennedy's vision so exited the scientists at the space agency about the prospects of actually making it happen 'during their watch' that they eventually fulfilled it.

The visions of the four not-for-profit organizations described in Appendices 1 to 4 are all aspirational in nature. Each has been cited for playing a major role in helping their respective organizations achieve the success they currently enjoy (as determined through a variety of performance outcome measures—See Question 15.) The visions are:

- ✓ To have everyone passionate about Theatre Capricorn (Theatre Capricorn)
- ✓ To be the place to be! (The Prairie Club)
- ✓ To stop the degradation of the planet's natural environment and build a future in which humans live in harmony with nature (Save the World Foundation), and
- ✓ Through our culture of caring and discovery, St. Alexandra's Hospital will be our nation's finest health care provider (St. Alexandra's Hospital).

By their nature as aspirational statements, great visions generally take a long time to realize. Like Kennedy's challenge to NASA in the 1960s, for example, it is not unusual for a vision to take a minimum of 10 years to realize. Directors should, therefore, ensure that their organization's vision involves a suitable time frame for its achievement.

Finally, visions that are explicit, clear and widely shared have a powerful and positive impact on internal stakeholders, such as employees and volunteers. The more committed these individuals are to seeing their organization's vision achieved, the more their collective spirit will serve to reinforce desired behaviours and focus both individual and group efforts on achieving desired outcomes. Consequently, directors should assure themselves that their organization's vision is widely known, understood—and accepted—throughout the organization.

13. Does the strategy have the right mission?

A mission statement is a formal written document that describes an organization's unique and enduring purpose and practices. In particular, it should answer the most fundamental question of organizational purpose: Why do we exist?

Generally speaking, organizations exist when they are able to continuously meet and satisfy the needs of those important stakeholders who have a significant influence on the organization and its sustainability. A not-for-profit's stakeholders can include users/beneficiaries, applicants, customers, paid employees/staff, volunteers, funders (i.e. owners, members, government departments, donors) or even society-at-large. The better the organization identifies, meets and satisfies its stakeholders' needs, the more likely it will be able to secure the long-term loyalty and support of each stakeholder and the greater the probability of the organization's ongoing success and prosperity.

Therefore, a mission is the essential platform that helps transport the organization towards it vision!

On the other hand, to the extent that a not-for-profit organization fails to satisfy a particular stakeholder group in a significant way, it risks alienating the commitment of that group to the organization and, even worse, goading them into an attack. This will most likely result in the failure of one or more goals and objectives and, under extreme conditions, can even lead to problems in organizational survival.

Directors must, therefore, ensure that the mission statement **acknowledges the importance of multiple stakeholder groups** to the organization's long-term survival and that it **balances their often competing interests**. However, it is especially important that the stakeholder needs specified in the mission be grounded in *reality*. The strategic plan should indicate the basis upon which the needs of each stakeholder group were identified and selected (such as through surveys or informal focus groups of various customers, employees, users, donors, etc.).

Although various methods may be used to identify stakeholders and their needs, this does not need to be a long, complicated or expensive exercise. Instead, it should be designed to quickly confirm, or deny, the instincts or perceptions of the board and management with respect to stakeholder needs.

Also, to the extent that a significant funder's needs change, the not-for-profit organization must determine whether it will re-orient itself to those changed needs (and, therefore, change its mission) or, instead, seek replacement funders whose interests are more closely aligned with those of its current users or beneficiaries.

Finally, as is the case with an organization's vision, mission statements should be explicit, clear and widely shared if they are to have a powerful and positive impact on internal stakeholders' behaviours. Accordingly, directors need to assure themselves that people throughout the organization are aware of, understand and accept the organization's mission.

The problem with measurement is its seeming simplicity.

—Anon.

14. Does the strategy have a proper statement of values?

Every organization needs to be sure that the actions and behaviours of its employees, volunteers and others can withstand the test of public scrutiny.

Values constitute the internal ethical and cultural priorities that shape the way people behave and make decisions. When values, such as honesty, mutual respect, transparency, innovation, teamwork, commitment, etc., are widely shared, they enhance the not-for-profit's ability to focus the behaviour of its employees and volunteers. Organizations can also use their statements of values and codes of conduct as vehicles for attracting the right stakeholders to them.

Directors of not-for-profit organizations should, therefore, ensure that their organization's strategy contains a statement of the values which they consider to be important for the harmonious and ethical running of their operations.

15. Does the strategy contain S.M.A.R.T. objectives that are well formulated and well stated?

Organizations use **objectives** to measure and judge their progress in achieving *the goals embedded in their mission, vision and values*. These objectives may be of a qualitative or quantitative in nature.

Quantitative objectives typically deal with expected "deliverables" that can be counted, such as financial results or other 'outcome activities', such as the number of people who are expected to attend an event. **Qualitative objectives**, on the other hand, deal with stakeholders' opinions and feelings. However, these must also be expressed numerically (such as a customer satisfaction score). As a general rule, objectives should be established for each goal *contained within the organization's mission, vision and values.*

For example, one of The Prairie Club's goals to achieve its mission is "to provide the highest quality and service experience that consistently exceeds member and guest expectations." The Club has decided to measure its progress towards achieving that goal through various surveys of its members and guests with the objective of scoring 5 out of 5 on customer satisfaction ratings. Other examples of objectives and their connection with an organization's mission are presented in Appendices 1 to 4.

To be effective, though, an organization's objectives must be both well formulated and well stated. These are known as S-M-A-R-T objectives:

- ✓ Specific (there is no ambiguity as to what the organization is trying to accomplish)
- ✓ Measurable (it is possible to determine whether the objectives has been achieved or not)

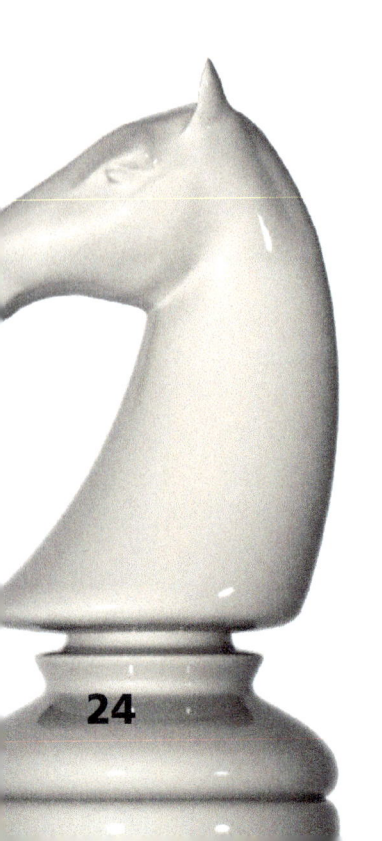

- ✓ Acceptable (the measures selected for tracking progress against the mission, vision and values are perceived as fair and appropriate)
- ✓ Realistic (they reflect reality and are motivational—i.e., capable of spurring commitment from employees, volunteers, donors and others), and
- ✓ Timely (as the great economist, Lord Keynes, once said: "In the long run, we are all dead!")

Regarding this last point, detailed organizational objectives are best stated for a time period of one to three years. They should also be revised at the end of each year as new information becomes available.

Also, determining whether an objective is realistic or not involves considerable judgment and skill. A key concern, therefore, is whether the people who will be responsible for achieving the specific targets contained in the objectives perceive those targets to be realistic. To do this, directors first need to understand the basis upon which the objectives were established (e.g., customer, user, donor, etc. surveys; benchmarking studies, etc.) They must also determine whether the objectives **balance** the conditions in the external environment with the organization's internal capabilities (for a further discussion of this, see question 16).

Finally, organizations should also conduct internal surveys of their employees and volunteers to determine *how well they understand and accept* the high-level objectives that will be used to measure the organization's progress in implementing its mission, vision and values. When people feel connected to their organization's strategic objectives, they typically work more diligently towards achieving those objectives and are more committed to the organization. Therefore, directors should assure themselves that the organizational objectives are effectively translated, disseminated and aligned throughout the organization—especially to the front line. To be sure, this can be a time consuming and daunting exercise and so it may be best—particularly in smaller organizations—to phase in the alignment of objectives over time.

If you have boarded the wrong train, it is of no use running along the corridor in the opposite direction.

—Anon.

16. Are the "scope of activities" specified in the organization's strategy the right ones?

Organizations should strive to focus their resources **only** on those products, services, benefits or assistance activities—as well as target groups—where:

- ✓ favourable external market, community, or societal conditions exist for the organization to achieve its stated mission, vision and values (this is called an 'opportunity') and

> **Without competitors there would be no need for strategy, for the sole purpose of strategic planning is to enable the organization to gain, as effectively as possible, a sustainable edge over its competitors.**
>
> —Kenichi Ohmae

✓ the organization has the internal resources—either on hand or quickly available—to pursue and capture the opportunity.

If either or both of these conditions do not exist, the organization faces the difficult challenge of determining *if and how* the situation might be turned around and made more favourable. Alternatively, it may have to acknowledge the brutal reality that the organization no longer needs to exist and should be wound up.

This is the *essential discipline* that boards need to apply when assessing their organization's strategy.

Making "scope of activity" selections is generally regarded as one of the most demanding—and important—processes in formulating or evaluating an organization's strategy. It involves the most amount of information gathering and typically represents the bulk of where strategic planning efforts should be placed.

Asking the following questions *for each activity and domain selection* will help directors assess the external market conditions and internal capabilities associated with their organization's scope of activities:

✓ What is the nature and extent of demand for the activity (i.e. products, services, benefits or assistance) offered?
✓ To what extent, and in what way, are the needs of customers, users, clients or target audiences for the activity currently being met by existing providers?
✓ To what extent are the organization's products, services, benefits or assistance activities significantly differentiated from—and offer a clear distinction over—those of other providers?
✓ Does the organization have the resources, skills and capabilities required to meet the potential demand that has been identified in its activity selections or target audiences?
✓ If it lacks a distinctive advantage or any specific resources, skills or capabilities, is the organization able to acquire the advantage/resources it needs, either on its own or in collaboration or partnership with others?
✓ What are the major assumptions underlying the choice of each major activity or target group selection?
✓ What is the relative importance of each activity and target group selection?

Strategy Implementation Considerations

17. Have the proper organizational arrangements been selected, designed and aligned to reflect, reinforce and support the not-for-profit organization's strategy?

Given sufficient time, information and human intelligence, *any* organization is capable of designing an outstanding strategy. The tough part occurs when it comes to executing it—i.e, *turning the strategy into a reality*.

One of the major ways in which execution happens is through the organization's operating plan, as discussed under Question 9.

The other major method by which organizations execute their strategies is by aligning their paid and volunteer staff, structures and control systems to focus on, support and reinforce the organization's strategic goals and objectives. This is called **strategic organizational alignment** and it entails four major considerations of concern to directors.

First, the mission, vision, values and objectives must be expressed in terms that are meaningful and understood by all members of the organization. This is necessary if they are to put forward a united and concerted effort towards realizing the strategy. Often, this will require redefining or re-specifying employees' and volunteers' jobs in a way that *reflects the strategy's requirements*. Committees, task forces and other working groups in the organization will also need to make sure their work addresses and contributes to the aims and aspirations contained in the strategy. These particular alignment activities should be conducted at least annually.

Second, individuals to be hired by the organization should be recruited primarily on the basis of their ability to perform the critical tasks and priorities *specified in the strategy*. And when the strategy has changed, existing employees should be retrained to better align their skills and activities with it.

Third, information systems should be adjusted to regularly measure and report on the organization's progress against all aspects of its strategy (especially the S.M.A.R.T. objectives) as well as the contributions individual members make towards its achievement. After all, timely, accurate and *"strategy focused" information* is necessary if the organization is to be able to assess the effectiveness of its operating plans and individuals' specific job behaviours—and then modify them, if necessary, to better achieve the strategy before it's too late.

Finally, the fourth element of organizational alignment demands that the not-for-profit adjust its recognition system so that employees and volunteers are acknowledged and rewarded ONLY for the "right" efforts—i.e., *those that contribute to helping the organization realize its*

> *The execution of the laws is more important than the making of them.*
>
> —Thomas Jefferson, 3rd President of the United States

strategy. Interestingly, recognizing people in this manner inspires and motivates them to put even greater efforts into making the strategy happen.

When key organizational structures and systems have been **aligned** as described above, the probability of a not-for-profit organization achieving its strategic goals and objectives will be greatly enhanced. (For an insightful and novel understanding of how organizations can easily create the kind of *organizational alignment* needed for better success at implementing their missions, readers are encouraged to consider the best selling book, *A Tale of Two Employees and the person who wanted to lead them*—also by the author.)

Assessing Strategic Risks

18. Have all the significant internal and external strategic risks facing the not-for-profit organization been identified, quantified and addressed in the strategic plan?

With any strategy, some *uncertainty* always exists around its ultimate attainment.

And with uncertainty comes *risk*—i.e. possible events that, should they occur, would adversely affect the organization and its ability to achieve its objectives. Some risks have a greater likelihood of occurring than others, but the presence of any of them can significantly alter the opportunities the organization is able to pursue, the weaknesses it is trying to overcome, the way certain organizational arrangements are made or the success the organization has in achieving objectives related to its mission, vision and values.

For this reason, directors must be sure they understand all of the risks associated with a particular strategy, the *probability* or likelihood of these risks occurring and the *potential impact* each risk may have on the organization. One way of doing this is by ensuring that the organization has in place an effective risk management system that identifies, measures and monitors known risks, estimates their impact, mitigates their occurrence or effect (e.g., through insurance, avoidance, codes of conduct or assigned risk managers), and identifies emerging dangers.

Another useful way for managing risks occurs as a result of the method by which directors are chosen to serve on the board. When correctly screened and selected, the individual and collective experiences and backgrounds of the directors provide a boardroom context in which they can properly understand, assess and help mitigate the risks facing their organizations.

Organizations, of course, face many different types of potential risk.

However, the main strategic risks of concern to not-for-profit boards parallel those which are *related to and drive its strategy*. These include risks that:

- ✓ stated objectives will not be realized
- ✓ opportunities perceived to exist with respect to realizing the mission, vision, values and objectives will not materialize (e.g. because of changes in demand or satisfaction levels related to customers, users, donors, beneficiaries and other target audiences, or changes in regulations etc.)
- ✓ internal resources necessary to realize the strategy will either disappear or cannot reasonably be secured (e.g., the loss of key employees/volunteers, a decline in organization morale, the inability to innovate, a failure of marketing initiatives, the occurrence of fraud and asset theft, etc.), and
- ✓ organizational arrangements chosen to implement the strategy do not function as intended.

Each of these risks should be spelled out in the strategic plan. And, directors should approve only those strategies where the associated risks—and their impact—are considered to be tolerable *given the potential for success*.

Monitoring Progress

19. **Are appropriate mechanisms in place to provide the board with timely feedback on the not-for-profit organization's progress against its strategy, the underlying causes of any performance variance and any changes in the internal/external environments or risk factors which would cause the board to consider altering the organization's strategy?**

Once the organization's strategy is approved and its supporting operational plan begins to be implemented, directors have a responsibility for monitoring the organization's *progress in achieving its strategic objectives*. Consequently, a review of the organization's progress against each of its strategic objectives—together with an update on any significant organizational risks—should be undertaken regularly during meetings of the full board.

> *The first step in the risk management process is to acknowledge the reality of risk. Denial is a common tactic that substitutes deliberate ignorance for thoughtful planning.*
>
> —Charles Tremper

Another Word About 'Constructive Involvement' and Who Does What

The board's responsibility to actively participate in developing and approving their organization's overall strategy, monitoring the strategy's progress, and overseeing and guiding the organization are **quintessential activities of good governance**—whether for-profit or not-for-profit.

Many not-for-profit boards are already actively involved in this area. Others may only be beginning to take on these tasks and duties. As they do, it will create a shift both in their role and manner in which they interact with management—especially the CEO or Executive Director.

As this document has described, senior executives have an important role to play in developing an organization's strategy—but it is not an exclusive role. Unfortunately, many not-for-profit senior executives will view the board's new strategic responsibilities as incursions into decision areas that were once strictly within their domain. Boards should, therefore, be prepared—and anticipate—encountering *potential resistance from senior managers* as the board becomes more involved in participating in the organization's strategic decision making.

Good boards and their managements, however, must reach a common agreement on the responsibilities of each, since it is in no one's best interests if the relationship between the board and senior management becomes adversarial—especially when setting the organization's future direction.

Boards, therefore, should work diligently to create a positive relationship with management and, to assess this, need to ask:

20. Is our board constructively involved in the not-for-profit organization's strategy?

A first step in building a relationship of constructive involvement with management is for the board to have an open and candid discussion with the CEO/Executive Director (and other members of senior management) about the new governance responsibilities the board requires in terms of the organization's strategy. Ultimately, the board and management must come to an understanding and agreement as to:

- ✓ who does what, in terms of formulating, assessing and approving the organization's strategy and strategic plan
- ✓ what areas constitute strategic—or board—decisions, and
- ✓ what areas represent operational/tactical—or management—decisions.

All of these responsibilities should be spelled out in a **Board Charter**.

Senior managers especially need to understand that the board's new tasks with respect to strategy are not being taken because of a lack of confidence in the organization's leadership. Rather, they are part of the **new stewardship role** that all boards are being asked to perform to avoid the two major governance mistakes of the past: boards that either 'rubber stamped' major management decisions (especially the organization's strategy) or tried to micro manage of the organization's operations.

Constructive involvement ultimately depends on the existence of a level of trust and mutual respect between the board and senior management. Not-for-profit directors must feel comfortable in asking strategic questions. And senior management must feel that they can be forthcoming in their responses to those questions.

Consequently, not-for-profit boards should conduct an **annual self-assessment** in the area of constructive involvement, possibly with a skilled facilitator, to help directors assess the degree of trust and respect that exists between them and management and to help sort out mutual responsibilities. Ideally, this should be part of a complete board governance assessment or review. And to the extent that problem areas are identified, the board could then consider what steps it next needs to take in order to correct the situation.

Appendices

The following five Appendices provide:

Examples of how different types of not-for-profit organizations have articulated their strategy according to the framework prescribed in this document (Appendices 1-4). The examples are presented for guidance purposes only and accordingly are illustrative rather than comprehensive in content; and

An example of the types of information that a complete strategic plan should contain. (Appendix 5)

APPENDIX 1:

Strategy at "Theatre Capricorn"

Mission

At Theatre Capricorn we deliver regional professional theatre at its best, focused on providing an exceptional life experience for patrons, employees, artists and volunteers.

We take pride in making theatre accessible to the broadest audience of all ages.

Our success and sustainability are measured through our creativity and innovation, our outreach and community support, our financial soundness and our development of young minds.

Let our passion fuel your imagination!

Vision

To have everyone passionate about Theatre Capricorn!

Values

- ✓ Personal Excellence (i.e. giving the best of ourselves in everything we do)
- ✓ Mutual respect
- ✓ Honesty
- ✓ Do it with Passion!

Objectives (One example only)

MISSION GOAL: To provide an exceptional life experience for patrons

Objectives

Over the 3 year life of the Plan:

- Increase box office sales 6%
- Increase subscriptions 10%
- Increase membership 15%
- Rating of >4 on regular customer satisfaction surveys

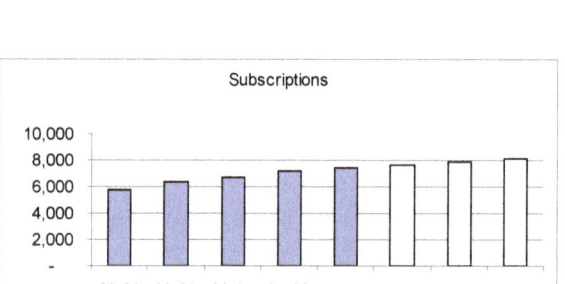

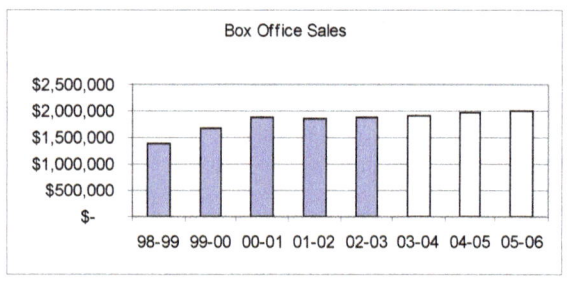

Scope of Activities

PRODUCTS:

- Main Stage (5 plays)
- Stage write series (3 plays)
- Special presentations (2)
- Holiday Family Musical (1)
- Classical Kids (1)
- The Lawyers' Show (1—alternating years)
- Brave New Works Festival
- Special Events
  - Behind the curtain
  - Vine Dining
- Community on Stage (Theatre rentals)
- Boutique
- Theatre School
- Activities for Educators
- Activities for Students
- Student matinees

MARKETS:

- Hamilton (82%)
- Greater Niagara (5%)
- Burlington (9%)
- Oakville (2%)
- Mississauga (1%)
- Toronto (1%)

APPENDIX 2:

Strategy at "The Prairie Club"

Mission

The Prairie Club, as a world-class private club, provides the highest quality and service experience, within a progressive environment, that consistently exceeds member and guest expectations.

Our home away from home is recognized as a place where friends gather to enhance their personal and business relationships through camaraderie, fellowship and diversity.

For Our Employees

Staff members share in the joy of the club because we provide a stable, challenging and rewarding work atmosphere.

Vision

To be the place to be in the Prairies!

Values

Excellent quality and service
Mutual respect
Honesty
Honour our traditions
Innovative, constant improvement

Objectives (One example only)

MISSION GOAL: To provide the highest quality and service experience that consistently exceeds member and guest expectations.

Objective:

Score 5 out of 5 on customer satisfaction ratings related to this mission goal by 2012 using the measurement methods listed below.

Measurement methods:

1. Member survey (cards on table) asking members:
   a. "How satisfied are you with:
      - ✓ *the quality of the Club's food and beverage products that you have just enjoyed?"*
      - ✓ the 'service experience' at the Club?"
   b. "To what extent does the Club:
      - ✓ consistently exceed your expectations?"
      - ✓ provide good value?"
2. Event survey asking the same questions PLUS: "To what extent are you satisfied with the overall quality of the event that you have just experienced at the club?"
3. Annual member survey related to the same questions.

Scope of Activities

PRODUCTS & SERVICES OF THE PRAIRIE CLUB

Weekday breakfasts	Casino night
Weekday luncheons	Guest speaker series
Weekday dinners	The Main Bar—downstairs
Special events—general	The Meeting Room
Chef's table	The Card Room
Members Table at lunch	The Games Room
Monthly Sunday brunch	The Library collection
Art appreciation night	The Library/Reading Room
Wine tasting events	Reciprocal arrangements

APPENDIX 3:

Strategy at "Save the World Foundation"

Vision

To stop the degradation of the planet's natural environment and to build a future in which humans live in harmony with nature.

Mission

The Mission of the Save the World Foundation is:
- ✓ To conserve the world's biological diversity
- ✓ To ensure that the use of renewable natural resources is sustainable
- ✓ To promote the reduction of pollution and wasteful consumption
- ✓ To provide our staff and volunteers with the opportunity to develop personally and professionally in a respectful, open environment that frequently recognizes honesty, teamwork, individual accomplishment and innovation
- ✓ To be the pride of our world community. When STWF succeeds, we succeed as individuals, and we contribute to the success of our planet.

Objectives (One example only)

MISSION GOAL: To conserve the world's biological diversity.

Objectives

1. Within 3 years, save the critically endangered Pacific leatherbacks from extinction by restoring their population to 100,000
2. Within 2 years, ensure the recovery of Western Atlantic leatherbacks to 250,000
3. Within 1 year, maintain hawksbill genetic diversity and secure their recovery
4. Within 2 years, ensure the recovery of the Eastern Pacific green turtle to sustainable levels of 1,000,000.

Scope of Activities

SPECIES SCOPE:

a. Turtles (10 species)

b. Whales (20 species)

c. Rain forests (32 locations)

SPECIES TARGET REGIONS:

a. Latin America

b. Caribbean

c. Asia

d. Antarctic

APPENDIX 4:

Strategy at "St. Alexandra's Hospital"

"Unless a variety of opinions are laid before us, we have no opportunity of selection, but are bound of necessity to adopt the particular view which may have been brought forward"

—Herodotus, 5th century BC

Vision

St. Alexandra's Hospital, through its culture of caring and discovery, will be our nation's finest academic health care provider.

Mission

St. Alexandra's Hospital is an academic health care provider and committed to innovative patient care, teaching and research. Established in 1920, St. Alexandra's Hospital remains dedicated to treating all with respect, compassion and dignity.

At St. Alexandra's Hospital, we recognize the value of every person and are guided by our commitment to excellence and leadership. We demonstrate this by our MISSION of:

- ✓ Providing exemplary physical, emotional and spiritual care for each of our patients and their families
- ✓ Balancing the continued commitment to the care of the poor and those most in need with the provision of highly specialized services to a broader community
- ✓ Building a work environment where each person is valued, respected and has an opportunity for personal and professional growth
- ✓ Advancing excellence in health services education
- ✓ Fostering a culture of discovery in all of our activities and supporting exemplary health sciences research

- ✓ Strengthening our relationships with universities, colleges, other hospitals, agencies and our community
- ✓ Demonstrating social responsibility through the just use of our resources

The commitment of our staff, physicians, volunteers, students, community partners and friends to our mission permits us to maintain a 'quality of presence' and 'tradition of caring', which are the hallmarks of St. Alexandra's Hospital.

Objectives (One example only)

MISSION GOAL: Providing exemplary physical, emotional and spiritual care for each of our patients and their families.

> **Objective 1a.** = score 95 OUT OF 100 in terms of Patient Experience "Overall Care—Emergency" by 2012
>
> **Objective 1b.** = Over 90% of patients state they had a positive ER experience. This is above the GTA Peer 3 ER comparison group.
>
> **Definition:** The percentage of patients who had a positive experience in the A-site or B-site Emergency Departments. Patients are surveyed using the Picker Institute Dimensions of Patient Centered Care.
>
> **Objective 2a.** = score 98 OUT OF 100 in terms of Patient Experience "Overall Care—Acute Care, In-patients" by 2012
>
> **Objective 2b.** = Over 90% of Acute Care In-patients rate their experience as positive.
>
> **Definition** = Percentage of Acute Care In-patients (Cardiac, Medical, Surgical & Neuro/MSK) who indicate they had an overall positive experience with their care based on the Picker Institute's Dimensions of Patient Centered Care.
>
> **Objective 3a.** = score 99 OUT OF 100 in terms of Patient Experience "Overall Care—Rehabilitation Services" by 2012
>
> **Objective 3b.** = Over 90% of Rehabilitation In-patients rate their experience as positive.
>
> **Definition** = Percentage Rehabilitation In-patients who indicate they had an overall positive experience with their care based on the Picker Institute's Dimensions of Patient Centered Care.

Scope of Activities

SERVICES	TARGET GROUPS							
	Cardiac	Children	Chest	Cancer	Mentally Disordered	Diabetes	Acquired Brain Damage	Adolescents	Other
1. Treatment									
2. Rehabilitation Services									
3. Prolonged Care									
4. Research									
5. Training and Education									
6. Program Consultation									
7. Provincial Resource									

APPENDIX 5:

Strategic Plans and Planning

A **Strategic Plan** is a document that records decisions made by the organization with respect to its future strategy, including the rationales, analyses and background information that support those decisions. Good strategic planning processes facilitate the creation of a superior strategy and ensure that the appropriate information is contained in the plan. Information typically included in a strategic plan includes:

Vision, Mission and Values

(S.M.A.R.T.) Objectives (related to the mission, vision and values)

Scope of Activities Selections (for achieving the mission, vision, values and objectives)

External Environmental Analysis to assess the potential for achieving the S.M.A.R.T. objectives in selected activities

- Political, economic, technological and social demographics analysis
- Market research (formal and/or informal) **related to** identifying and satisfying (current and unmet) stakeholder (i.e., donor, customer/user, benefactor, volunteer, societal, etc.) needs
- Potential 'target audience' demand/growth/profitability
- Number and type of alternative providers
- Relative positioning of alternative providers and their degree of product/service/benefit/assistance differentiation
- Barriers to entry/exit
- 'Switching costs' related to customers/users and donors
- Industry benchmarks and performance standards

Internal Resource Analysis to assess the organization's ability to achieve its S.M.A.R.T. objectives in selected activities

- ✓ Strengths and weaknesses analysis **related to** achieving goals and objectives and increasing superior differentiation
- ✓ Analysis of capabilities for innovation
- ✓ Donor/owner satisfaction survey results
- ✓ Customer/user satisfaction survey results
- ✓ Employee satisfaction survey results
- ✓ Gap analysis results relative to desired 'outcomes'
- ✓ Key success factors
- ✓ Plans for overcoming critical weaknesses or strengthening advantages

Methods of entry into (or exit from) major activities and domain selections

Risk Analysis

- ✓ Major risks (internal and external)
- ✓ Risk impact analysis e.g. sensitivity analysis
- ✓ Risk impact outcomes—including best and worst cases
- ✓ Risk management/abatement tactics

Assumptions

- ✓ Qualitative
- ✓ Quantitative

Major Strategic Alternatives

- ✓ A summary of major changes represented in the proposed/future strategy in relation to the strategy currently in use
- ✓ Descriptions of major strategic alternatives that were rejected and the rationale for their rejection

Strategic Organizational Alignment/Strategy Implementation

- ✓ Organization chart
- ✓ Major changes in job definitions, information systems, and human resource practices (paid and volunteer) in order to bring them into alignment with the strategy
- ✓ Succession plan for key management/board positions
- ✓ Potential areas of resistance to change—and methods for overcoming them
- ✓ Links between the strategic and operating plans

Financial and other measurements

- ✓ The projected financial impact of the proposed/future strategy for at least 3 years.
- ✓ Key performance indicators
- ✓ Milestones

20 Questions Workbook

On the following pages, you'll find the 20 questions with space for you to write your own response. Feel free to photocopy these pages so that you can update them from time to time.

1. How is strategy defined at this organization?
2. What are we ultimately trying to accomplish (currently) and where do we eventually want to get to? (The Vision Goal)
3. What is our current purpose—or, why do we exist? (The Mission Goals)
4. What are the current internal ethical and cultural ("how we do things around here") priorities that attract stakeholders to us? (The Values Goals)
5. What are the specific measures and targets that we use to judge our progress in achieving our vision, mission and values goals? (The Objectives)
6. What specific product, service, benefit or assistance activities have we currently chosen to focus on and, to which specific group(s) (or markets) have we chosen to offer them for the purposes of achieving our objectives? (The Scope of Activities and Domain Selections)
7. Is the definition of strategy in this not-for-profit organization shared by all directors and management?
8. What are the major business strategies that make up the not-for-profit's organizational strategy?
9. Do circumstances warrant the board's involvement in (i.e. reviewing, assessing and approving) the organization's operating plan?
10. Does this not-for-profit organization have the right strategy and, if not, what should it be?
11. What process was used to formulate the strategy contained in the not-for-profit's strategic plan and does the plan's document contain all of the proper information?
12. Does the strategy have the right vision?
13. Does the strategy have the right mission?
14. Does the strategy have a proper statement of values?
15. Does the strategy contain S.M.A.R.T. objectives that are well formulated and well stated?
16. Are the "scope of activities" specified in the organization's strategy the right ones?
17. Have the proper organizational arrangements been selected, designed and aligned to reflect, reinforce and support the not-for-profit organization's strategy?
18. Have all the significant internal and external strategic risks facing the not-for-profit organization been identified, quantified and addressed in the strategic plan?
19. Are appropriate mechanisms in place to provide the board with timely feedback on the not-for-profit organization's progress against its strategy, the underlying causes of any performance variance and any changes in the internal/external environments or risk factors which would cause the board to consider altering the organization's strategy?
20. Is our board constructively involved in the not-for-profit organization's strategy?

1. How is strategy defined at this organization?

_____
_____
_____
_____

2. What are we ultimately trying to accomplish (currently) and where do we eventually want to get to? (The Vision Goal)

_____
_____
_____
_____

3. What is our current purpose—or, why do we exist? (The Mission Goals)

_____
_____
_____
_____

4. What are the current internal ethical and cultural ("how we do things around here") priorities that attract stakeholders to us? (The Values Goals)

_____
_____
_____

5. What are the specific measures and targets that we use to judge our progress in achieving our vision, mission and values goals? (The Objectives)

6. What specific product, service, benefit or assistance activities have we currently chosen to focus on and, to which specific group(s) (or markets) have we chosen to offer them for the purposes of achieving our objectives? (The Scope of Activities and Domain Selections)

7. Is the definition of strategy in this not-for-profit organization shared by all directors and management?

8. What are the major business strategies that make up the not-for-profit's organizational strategy?

_____
_____
_____
_____

9. Do circumstances warrant the board's involvement in (i.e. reviewing, assessing and approving) the organization's operating plan?

_____
_____
_____
_____

10. Does this not-for-profit organization have the right strategy and, if not, what should it be?

_____
_____
_____
_____

11. What process was used to formulate the strategy contained in the not-for-profit's strategic plan and does the plan's document contain all of the proper information?

12. Does the strategy have the right vision?

13. Does the strategy have the right mission?

14. Does the strategy have a proper statement of values?

53

15. Does the strategy contain S.M.A.R.T. objectives that are well formulated and well stated?

16. Are the "scope of activities" specified in the organization's strategy the right ones?

17. Have the proper organizational arrangements been selected, designed and aligned to reflect, reinforce and support the not-for-profit organization's strategy?

18. Have all the significant internal and external strategic risks facing the not-for-profit organization been identified, quantified and addressed in the strategic plan?

___

19. Are appropriate mechanisms in place to provide the board with timely feedback on the not-for-profit organization's progress against its strategy, the underlying causes of any performance variance and any changes in the internal/external environments or risk factors which would cause the board to consider altering the organization's strategy?

___

20. Is our board constructively involved in the not-for-profit organization's strategy?

___

About the author

Dr. Chris Bart is the **world's leading authority** on organizational mission and vision statements. He is the **Founder, Principal and Lead Professor of The Directors College**, Canada's first university accredited corporate director certification program. Dr. Bart is also the author of the Canadian business best seller, *A Tale of Two Employees and the Person Who Wanted to Lead Them* as well as the widely acclaimed CICA publication, *20 Questions Directors Should Ask About Strategy, Second Edition*.

Through his pioneering research and teachings, Dr. Bart has become highly sought after by organizations seeking to develop vision and mission statements that get results. His practical approach for bringing mission statements to life has inspired business leaders and audiences around the world.

As a **Professor of Strategic Market Leadership (Strategy and Governance)** at McMaster University's DeGroote School of Business, Dr. Bart has published over 100 articles, cases and reviews. He currently serves as **Associate Editor** of the **International Journal of Business Governance & Ethics**. He is also an **innovator**. He helped establish the Management of Innovation and New Technology Research Centre at McMaster and was its first Director. Later, he devised and created the Innovation Management Network: a worldwide association of academics and practitioners who collaborate through the internet on matters of innovation and new technology.

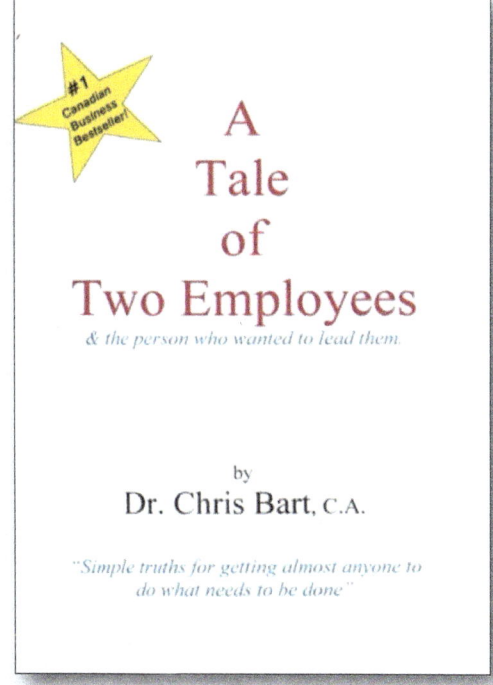

Dr. Bart has been awarded the **Ontario Chamber of Commerce Outstanding Business "Achievement Award for Corporate Governance"**, **the Hamilton Chamber of Commerce "HR Hero Award"**, **the United Way "Chairman's Award" and McMaster's "Innovation Award"**. A highly regarded lecturer, Dr. Bart has received both the **"Outstanding Undergraduate Business Professor"** and **"MBA Professor of the Year"** awards on multiple occasions. He has also won **"The President's Award for Teaching Excellence"**, McMaster's highest teaching award—which made him the most decorated professor at the DeGroote School. In 2009, his CA designation was elevated to **FCA** (Fellow of the Institute of Chartered Accountants).

Over the years, Dr. Bart has been invited to lecture at numerous institutions throughout the world, including South Africa, Switzerland, the United Kingdom, Australia, the Czech Republic and China.

Dr. Bart is listed in **Canadian Who's Who** and has been a director on many Boards.

Dr. Chris Bart, FCA
Corporate Missions Inc.
1063 King Street West, Suite 230
Hamilton, ON Canada L8S 4S3
(905) 308-8455
chrisbart@corporatemissionsinc.com
www.corporatemissionsinc.com

CPSIA information can be obtained
at www.ICGtesting.com
Printed in the USA
LVOW05s1501100416
482969LV00030B/729/P